Search Engine Optimization Guide

By Leland Dieno
www.dienodigital.ca
Copyright 2018
2018 edition
Version 1.1

Introduction

Search Engine Optimization has changed the modern world. Marketers and digital specialists are forever monitoring major search engines like Google as they update their algorithms to ensure that people utilizing their platforms to find products and services are provided with the most accurate information possible.

But SEO has grown to be so much more than that. The simple logic of optimizing any content that lives anywhere online has become a necessity.

From building internal "intranets" and databases, to ensuring that your LinkedIN profile has been optimized so that recruiters can find you has become critical for making any user experience valuable.

External SEO matters just as much as internal, and optimizing content for the best search results not only keeps us thinking about everything we write, but also developers across the world are having to ensure their platforms are optimized.

When a podcaster puts out a new episode of their podcast they need to make sure that a new listener may stumble across them by searching for the keyword or subject of that episode.

When a business lists a new product on amazon they have to figure out how to write their product descriptions so that potential customers can find them.

When an online grocery company is building an ecommerce platform to sell groceries, they need to ensure that their product inventory has appropriate descriptions and that within their own business model products are competing properly for search results.

When an institution is selling education, they need to make sure that when prospective students are searching for a program to study they are able to find the appropriate program, but also programs that they may be interested in.

Gas stations have to ensure that they are properly listed in Itunes and Google Maps because their next customer might be pulled over down the block searching for the nearest gas station as they are about to run out of gas.

Search Engine Optimization has changed marketing.

I have been developing websites since I was a teenager. In the late 90's getting your website listed on yahoo.com was much different than how difficult optimizing web content for the best search results is today.

These are just some of the tactics that I have learned throughout the years that have proven to work for me.

It's important to note that Google and other search engines are constantly, and will forever be updating their algorithms to ensure people who are "doing the searching" are being provided with the best possible information.

These tips and information is important to note, but the most critical thing you should be aiming to do with your content is to provide the most value possible for anyone who is looking for your content. A lot of "BlackHat" marketing tips can be used to quickly get traffic to a website and probably even increase sales, but for longevity and long term authority on a specific subject, quality will always win.

This is intended to be a quick "guide" and an easy read.

Exact Match Domains

There have been rumours and discussion that using an exact match domain no longer works. However, there is still credible evidence that exact match domains will still perform well if the site content is high quality.

My recommendation is to always try to include at least two of your primary keywords in your domain if you are building a site that is to strictly perform or obtain traffic on organic search results.

Example:

www.paulsplumbingservices.com for keywords "Paul's Plumbing Services".
www.thebestdishsoap.com for keywords "The Best Dish Soap"

Always try to include your keyword in your name unless you are buying a domain that is strictly going to be used to promote your business or brand (ie, if you have an established company, or your name has nothing to do with the services or products your provide).

Keep in mind: my testing has proven that .com always wins on terms of search engine ranking,.

HTTPS

Search engines are regularly updating their algorithms to check if a website is secure. Your site will rank higher if it's running on HTTPs.

Ensure that you have set up your SSL certificate before you start building your site and that it is working properly.

Why does HTTPs matter? If you enable security on your site (an absolute must and requirement if you are handling any kind of online financial transactions) it's showing that you care about your customers data. Encryption ensures that the simple hacks can't be made to steal your customer or website visitors information.

Page URLS

It is important to use hyphenated page urls. This will ensure each of your keywords is listed in your URL.

Example.

If Paul's Plumbing Services offers a new service of "outdoor power washing" his new page to communicate the services on his website would look like this:

www.paulsplumbingservices.com/outdoor-power-washing

Keyword Fundamentals

Despite what digital marketing rumours you may have heard keywords are still the essential need in organic search optimization.

Your keyword should be in the title tag of all of your posts and pages for what you are trying to rank for.

A trick is, if possible, figuring out how you can use your keyword twice in your title. This isn't necessary, and should only be used when it makes sense. If it damages your brand or the quality of your content you should avoid it.

Your title tag should be in <h1> </h1> (heading 1) on your page.

It is absolutely essential that your primary keyword is in the first paragraph of your copy.

Headings

You should only have one <h1> </h1> tag on your page and that should be your page title.

You can have multiple <h2> - <h4> tags on your page.

Use headings <h1> through <h4> properly, and in order. Primarily meaning that your <H1> is at the top of your page and your next heading should be a <h2>. This could impact your writing.

Your page and post copy

LSI (Latent Semantic Indexing) **keywords are important.** LSI Keywords are keywords that are relevant to your primary keyword. Over time search engines have been compiling data on keywords that are related to each other and these are factored into your ranking.

Keyword Density is still important! Your keyword should equal to 1% - 1.5% of your total copy. Meaning if you have 100 words, you should mention your keyword at least once.

In some instances, you may need to have higher keyword density, but you need to ensure you aren't over doing it. In my opinion you should aim to never be over 2.5% keyword density.

1,000 - 1,300 words on a page has been determined as the "sweet spot".

Ensure that 51% of the copy on your page is unique. This means that if you copy an article or information from another website, you need to expand it on uniquely.

Images

Both the file name and "Alt" tag on your image should be your keyword, or include your primary keyword.

Alt tag stands for "Alt attribute" of an IMG file. Which is essentially just adding another attribute to your image file that is commonly indexed and shows up in your page's code.

Always try to use .png, .jpg or .gif image file extensions. Always avoid extensions such as .bmp, .tiff.

Compress your images if possible and reduce their file size, but maintain as high quality as possible.

Linking

Internal site links on your website can attribute to better ranking. This means that you have to think outside of just using your primary and secondary "navigation" menus.

Links within the body of your content (your copy) have a higher impact when it comes to SEO. You need to balance this with usability to ensure you are still providing users with a good experience and flow on your website.

Linking to your site from external (other) websites is still a high factor in how well your website ranks. This means that search engine algorithms still factor in whether or not other sites are linking to your pages. The more quality links you have from other websites, the better you will rank as that is proving you as an "Authority" on the subject matter related to your keyword(s).

Some key methods of obtaining link(backs) to your site are:
1. Obtaining press (news and media linking back to your site)
2. Register for link exchanges and directories related to your business (yellow pages, and other directory websites, etc…)
3. Utilize an agency that specializes in obtaining these "back links".

There are many services online that offer purchasable "Back links". While this method may quickly move your site up the ranks in google it has

also been found that over time you will be de-ranked due to the fact that these links are actually just spam. Some marketers are now saying that they are actually noticing google isn't ranking sites higher with these spam-typed back links.

It's best to avoid them. It may take longer for your site to rank well in search engines you want longevity not a quick win that may in fact negatively impact your SEO so much in the future you will need to start from scratch.

Social Media Impacts SEO

Nothing official will say that having social media profile pages will directly improve your search engine ranking, however it is important that you at the very least, have a Google My Business account and pages set up that ensure your business is registered on google maps.

Search Engine Platforms rank very well, so if your business name always has your primary keyword in it, it is a good idea to have business pages set up across social media networks.

Managing social media becomes the next big issue. Content is key, but it is not for everyone due to a lack of resources. While social media content management strategy is a completely different subject, think logically about social media and where your customers may be "searching" for products. Platforms like Pinterest are becoming go tos for people when it comes to figuring out what kind of products exist and where to buy them.

At a very minimum ensure your business is set up in google.

Open Graph Tags (OG)

Social Media platforms such as Facebook are now using a specific code (meta tag) to understand what image should be displayed on timelines and feeds, and what title and description correspond with that.

By default, many platforms will just pull what you have set as your title, but my recommendation is to ensure you have enabled some sort of mechanism to separately specify an OG image + title and description.

On CMS's this is quite easy, especially wordpress where you can quickly install an open graph plugin to handle this for you, if your website is stand alone or built another way you will need to ensure it is optimized for social media.

Youtube is the new Google

Youtube has over 30 million users daily and is becoming the "Go to" for searches. People are looking up how tos and product reviews every day on the platform.

It is definitely worth integrating youtube into your digital marketing strategy.

When it comes to SEO, make sure you are embedding your youtube videos into your pages or blog posts and ensuring your primary keywords are a part of your title. Youtube video descriptions should also be thoughtfully written with SEO in mind.

Your Sitemap Matters

If you've never heard of a sitemap, go to your favourite website and add /sitemap.xml to the end of the web address. I am willing to bet that you will end up viewing an XML page of code that you probably don't understand.

However, as difficult it is for the average person to decipher a sitemap it is critical to your website's search engine success.

A sitemap tells search engines where to look for your content and how your website is organized.

Time on page & Bounce Rate Matter

A newer ranking mechanism that has been implemented by google is quite interesting. Let's say Bob, a father of 4 and husband is need of emergency plumbing services because his toddler stuck a leggo down the toilet and flushed it.

He searches "24 hour plumbing service" and Paul's website comes up first with a link directly to his emergency services page and a contact number.

Paul's site was brought up first because google has noticed that over the past 6 months multiple users have searched for emergency plumbing services, they have clicked on his link and not come back to google searching for it again. This typically means that they found what they were looking for and Paul's Plumbing website provided them with quality information based on the keywords they entered.

A good way of thinking about this is basically that if people are clicking on to pages of your website and then leaving quickly, returning to google only to search again or try another link that was provided, it probably means they didn't find what they were looking for.

If someone "bounces" off of your web page and closes their browser this could be considered a successful search, but if they return to google looking for the same keyword they searched for previously they obviously didn't get a solution to their problem.

Analytics

It would be tough to find an actual statement from Google as to the fact that a google analytics implementation would help your search ranking, but that doesn't mean that you should rule it out. As more and more Search Engine Optimizers talk about the algorithm analyzing whether or not people stay on your page, return to your page, and spend time on your page(s) there must be some link to google that is solidifying this information. That's at least the mentality I have with my approach to "installing" it on a website.

Google Analytics is completely free and provides you with the standard Key Performance Indicators or metrics that you would rely on to measure your site's success, so it is definitely something you should install.

Google provides the service for free.
Google is steadily improving their algorithm for better search results.
It just makes sense to set it up, even if you are using another third party data tracking platform, I would strongly urge you to plant google's analytics code on your site's pages.

Mobile Friendly

Most websites over the past 5 years will report that at least 50% of their visitors are visiting on some sort of mobile device.

Mobile devices include tablets, cell phones and anything with a screen resolution that isn't that of a laptop, mac, or pc.

Google searches are often made on cell phones, especially if the search is location based and people are searching for a product or service while "on the go". Texting and mobile usage while driving is becoming illegal in many states and provinces, but that isn't stopping people from using voice activated search, or pulling over. Companies from Gas Stations to Dry Cleaners are regularly being searched for on mobile devices, and yours probably will be or is as well.

Your site needs to be fully responsive, and load quickly on mobile devices. Both of these major factors will contribute to whether or not your site is ranking well.

If you are building a new website make sure that your developer or theme is mobile friendly (responsive) and if your current site is not, it's time to start figuring out how to make it responsive!

Tip: Google is smart enough to know when a site is loading in responsive mode vs desktop mode on a mobile device. So even if you think your site loads fine on a phone, if it's not responsive it is hurting your ranking.

Google Webmaster Tools (Search Console)

www.google.com/webmastertools (or search google for "google search console").

Google has built a platform for website owners and marketers to manage their sitemaps and review search data.

This could be the most important platform or utility you use to monitor your website's search and related data. It is free and absolutely necessary.

Be sure to set up your website, add a sitemap and review your search data on a monthly basis as the platform will tell you when your website is coming up in searches, what keywords are relating to your site and how many people are clicking on them. This is a very quick way to monitor your website's SEO status.

Google Is Always Getting Smarter

If you plan on implementing a content strategy that relies on organic search traffic search engine optimization needs to be on your priority list. It's important to note that Google is forever and always updating their algorithm to provide better content to their users.

You need to have the mindset of providing the best possible result to people searching for your keywords. That should be the primary objective and key goal of your content optimization strategy.

You can't outsmart google's algorithm in the long run, you may be able to find ways to trick it quickly but I can guarantee you that in time you will be deranked due to algorithm changes.

It's like any other business, if you put a ton of budget into promotions and advertising but provide a crappy product or service eventually your luck will run out. Keep that in mind as you work on your SEO goals and strategy.

The On Page SEO Checklist

Web page's URL uses dashes and includes your keyword(s).	
Your Page's title should be as close to your keyword as possible, or at least include your keyword.	
H1 is only for the title	
Your page has a H2 and H3 sub heading somewhere in the copy and they are in order.	
Your page has between 1,000 and 1,300 words.	
51% or more of the copy on the page is original content.	
Any images added to page have a descriptive "Alt Tag" configured with keywords identified.	
You have configured OG tags for both a social media image and title + description	

The Website SEO Checklist

Your domain references one of your keywords or is an exact match domain.	
Your website has a dynamic sitemap (updates automatically when new pages are entered)	
Google Analytics is installed	
Google Webmaster Tools (Search Console) has been configured	
Website is fully responsive	
Website has been set up with HTTPS	

www.ingramcontent.com/pod-product-compliance
Lightning Source LLC
Chambersburg PA
CBHW070948220526
45471CB00007B/2937